Love, Death, and In Between

Martyna Dearing

To request permissions, contact the publisher at drewsbookstoreva@gmail.com
Paperback: 979-8-9889899-3-6

Edited by Georgina Tsang
Cover art by Elliana Esquivel
Author's portrait photo by Robert Nelson
Interior design by Martyna Dearing

Printed by IngramSpark

Published by
Drew's Bookstore
70 Main St, suite 22
Warrenton, VA 20186

drewsbookstoreva@gmail.com
drewsbookstore.com

Love, Death, and In Between

Martyna Dearing

To my body, my soul, and my mind,
For carrying me through all the hardships.
From being bullied as a child…
To losing the only love I ever had.
Thank you,
For trying so fucking hard.
I hope I made you proud.

Contents

Prologue 1

love

  - love is not a game 5

  - brooklyn, Andrew's song 7

  - modern love story 8

  - that first move 11

  - not away 12

  - inspired 14

  - Virginia is home 15

  - what is love? 16

  - life happens 18

  - love in the mirror 19

death

  - what do you see? 24

  - a letter to my teenage self 26

  - first time griever 27

  - 9/26/2022 30

  - last words 31

  - don't wait to love him 32

  - bam 34

  - drunk 35

  - tired 36

  - happy Tuesday 38

  - let's be together again 39

  - your love made me a writer 40

- denial 41

- happy ending 42

- prayers 43

- that lucky 44

- too hot to be a widow 45

- a bus ride to Masaya 47

- waiting 48

- beyond 49

- youth 50

- 10 year plan 51

in between
- 26 55

- Rupi Kaur knows me 57

- away 58

- friday at the office 60

- the choice 61

- london 64

- I'll use you for my poetry 66

- frustrated 67

- fuck bro code 68

- to all women I love 70

- dancing gypsy 72

- 27 73

- crAsh 74

- just another heartbreak 75

- she's art 77

Epilogue 79

Prologue

Maybe there's an alternative universe where I'm currently pregnant with our first baby, McKenzie. You come home every day and kiss me on my forehead and then you place a gentle kiss with your beautiful lips on my pregnant belly. Kenzie is a kicker which probably means she'll be just as wild and obnoxious as her parents. You make me tomato soup and grilled cheese and we watch InkMaster or some cooking shows together. Then I pass out on the couch until you're ready to go to sleep. You wake me up by lightly touching my cheek with your big hands and we head to bed together. I complain about brushing my teeth because I'm too sleepy but soon after I fall asleep in your arms again. Life is good. I can see it so clearly that it seems impossible it never happened.

love

When you know you know
No doubts, no games, no reason
Love is like treason
To your brain
If they love you
There's no other way
They'll do anything to stay

- love is not a game

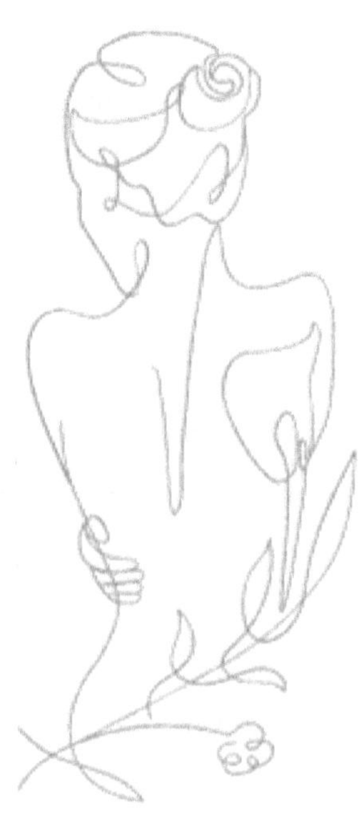

I fell in love in Brooklyn
Never thought that I could
But something about you girl
Made me think I should

We had so much pizza
On Knickerbrocker Avenue
And I had so much fun girl
But I realized it was because of you

Down on St. Patricks
And at the SoFar show
We traveled miles and miles
But baby I already know

I fell in love at the Brooklyn Bridge
We talked about our imaginary kids
Baby, I never thought that I could
But you made me think I should

Can't keep away from you
No matter how hard I try
There's something bout the way you feel
That makes me wanna get inside your heart

I fell in love
We talked about imaginary kids
And even though we may break up
You might be the one or not

Baby, I never thought that I could
But maybe we should

- *brooklyn, Andrew's song*

Halloween night
Have been drinking a lot
Swiped right on the app
He's coming over now

Red shirt
Dark hair
Blue jeans
Something's in the air
If you ask
I already know
He's the one
I don't have to look anymore.

Love at first sight
It was not
I fell in love
Way before that
The swipe
The text
The first time
We have met

The kiss
Our first night
The morning
just me in your arms.
All the other stuff
So unnecessary

With you by my side
Life isn't so scary.

First trip
First fight
First week without you
Just didn't feel right.

Memory after memory
Moment after moment
You said 'fuck it'
Got on your knee
And proposed out of nowhere
No rings
No wedding
All this stuff
So unnecessary

Thank you
I love you
Have a good day
I'll miss you

Simple words
Make all the difference
That's what being in love with you feels
Simple and different

No fancy cars
No expensive dinners
No tickets to Japan
No picket fence within a year

All this stuff
So unnecessary
From the first sight
I knew who I was gonna marry.

- modern love story

HAIKU

have your lips been kissed
he asks, won't move, standing still
I laugh, wait, then leave

                    - that first move

have your lips been kissed
he asks, won't move, standing still
I laugh, wait, then leave

I'm away
and you're not
You are home
and I'm far
I saw the world
and you didn't
I climbed the mountains
flew the skies
crossed the oceans
broke some hearts
Never understood
what family was
Never cared
never wanted
never needed at all
Then I met you
and my world turned
My heart aches
every time I'm away
every time I'm far
My heart's heavy
in my chest
in my mind
It's looking for you
my eyes blind
Then I come back
I open the door
and you're there
with three tails wagging
craving for our attention

Then we hug
we kiss
we fight
we love
and we fight some more
At some point
we're laying in a pile
with three tails wagging
then you smile
And now I know
I'm not away
I'm home

- not away

Inspired
To write poems
About madness
And the life that matters

Inspired
To fall in love
That takes your
Breath away

Inspired to breathe
Above the water
Taking it all in
Gasping for the fresh air

Inspired to use
The youth I was given
Trying not to waste
Another minute

Inspired to live
To the fullest
Like tomorrow could be my last day
And that would be okay.

- inspired

Oh Virginia
Like an old lover
Sometimes I forget
About your beauty
Sometimes I don't appreciate
Your people
You didn't raise me
But you raised the man
Who gave me his everything
You saw me growing
In love
Into a woman, I've become
You've seen the hurt
You've seen the tears
But at the end of the day
You made him
When life gets hard
Sometimes I forget
You gave me my everything
The love
And the tears
Oh Virginia
Thank you for the sunsets
For the sun rising
For my family
But mostly… for him

- Virginia is home

describe love
I can't
but then
I look into your eyes
and the things
I'm feeling
it's love
overwhelming
but safe

describe love
I can't
but then
you wrap your arms
around me
and the things
I'm feeling
it's love
like a blanket
keeping the evil
away

describe love
I can't
but then
I need you
I want you
I miss you
and I know

love is you
love is us
love is me
you changed my heart
I'll never live
a loveless life

to find
your soulmate
so young
in this loveless world
how lucky
we are
till the death
do us apart
and far far beyond…

- what is love?

HAIKU

love me like there's no
tomorrow like we have no
time left just say yes

- life happens

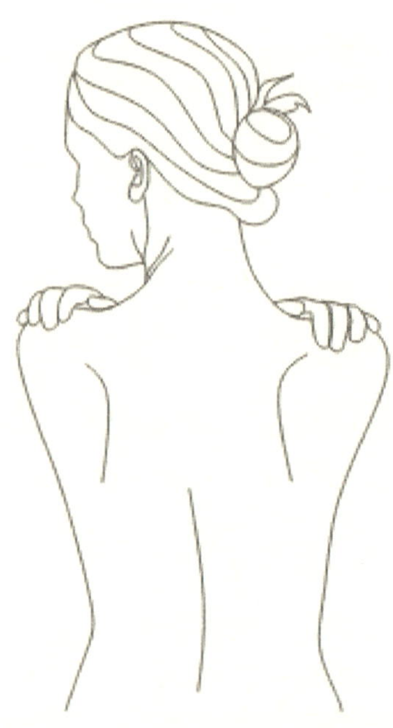

My whole adolescence I was told I was ugly
By my brother
By my mother
By my friends
And my bullies
I looked in the mirror and couldn't understand
What they saw in me
That I didn't see
looked at my beautiful face with my blue eyes -
and I kind of loved it
I looked at my body that carried me through the tough days -
and I kind of loved it
I looked at my hair that they said was from the witches -
and I kind of loved it
But they did everything to convince me I was wrong
That I shouldn't love the way I was
And for some time, I believed them
But I kept looking in the mirror
Wondering why I was the only one to see
The beauty in me
Until I met him
Not even once he questioned
Not even once he made me feel less
He spent every day
telling me how fucking beautiful I am
That I'm sexy
And hot
That my big booty
Made him respectfully hard

That no matter what
I'm the prettiest girl in the room
The way he loved me?
I realized that's what real love was
That's how we all should feel
Loved, secure, never doubting
Beautiful, hot, as fierce as lightning
So you go ahead and say I'm ugly
That I'm fucked up and broken
I can be all those things
But with his love
And with my soul
I'm so much fucking more
To him…
I'll always be
The most beautiful
Woman in the world

And to me?
I'm fucking unstoppable.

- love in the mirror

death

HAIKU

In the sky above
Privileged see just the clouds
We see our loved ones.

- what do you see?

A letter to my teenage self
Don't grow up
There's death
Everywhere
All the ones you love
They die
With no warning
With no words
You'll love deeply
But hurt even more
You'll find happiness
Just so it can be taken away.
Don't get attached
They'll leave
Don't fall in love
They're mortal
In one moment
They're your everything
But tomorrow
They don't even exist
To my teenage self
Believe me
We tried
We did our best
We thought we were right
Instead
We should've died
We should've never
Given the world
A chance to

Smash our hearts
There's only
That many times
A heart can break
Before it hopelessly
Stays apart.

- a letter to my teenage self

chaos
in my head
in my mind
they told me my dad is gone.
chaos in my mind
I don't know
if I know
he's not coming back
it feels like that
but then it does not.
chaos in my life
chaos at my home
I never feel alone.
marriage
career
family
and friends.
am I even there?
I'm not giving up
I don't think I am
but I'm not fighting either
so where do I stand?
fast paced life
routine
to do lists
errands
bills
goals unfulfilled.
I don't have time
we don't have money

there's an excuse for everything
honey.
my life is chaos
my dreams are gone
I feel stuck
I am stuck
so where is that girl?
I think she's gone.

- first time griever

I hope I die young
Unscarred by age
I hope I die young
Oblivious to pain

The moment of forgetting
The feeling of frustration
The pain of inability
The helpless infuriation

A loved one died young
Everyone says sorry
But instead I smile
Thinking of the days of his glory.
They didn't end
Till the moment of his last breath.

I hope I die young
Untouched by the disease
Full of life and smiles
Doing what I love
Leaving nothing behind
But love, kindness, and fond memories.

- 9/26/2022

You left
Your heart gave up
I'll always ask myself why it did
Did it give up on me
Did it give up on us
Or maybe it just happened
and there's no reason for it.

Your love
Your laugh
Your stupid jokes
Your kindness
Your passion
Your little dances
Your weird sexual comments
will never make my eyes roll again.

The world without you does not make sense
It barely exists…
You asked me if I could imagine my life without you
and I said nothing.
I really thought I could.
Little did I know there was nothing to imagine.
There's no life after you.

- last words

Nothing makes you more in love
Than him dying
Nothing makes you appreciate him
Like his absence
You want to be better
But why even bother?
He's gone
And nothing you do matters.

The memories flood your head
All day long
He's everywhere
Even where he's never been before.
He's in your dreams
You hug him
Never want to let go
You wake up
Alone
For the rest of your life
He's gone.

He's everywhere
But somehow not existing
He took his last breath
Taking all the air out of your system.

The regret consumes you
The blame shatters your heart.
You'd give anything
To turn back the clock.

Whatever happens
Doesn't really matter
He's gone
He took your heart
Fucked your life
Left you alone
Broke your soul
Tore everything you knew apart.

Now you're here
To pick up the pieces.
Heartless
Broken
Alone
Cleaning up all the messes.

- don't wait to love him

Bam!
Your life just felt apart
You're welcome to watch it
As it's quickly breaking into pieces
Shattered glass all over the floor.
So what's next, my friend?
Are you willing to hurt
picking up every shattered part?
Or are you gonna leave the mess behind?
In a foolish search for a new heart.

- bam

I find it quite impressive
how many tears I have left
Despite of the dehydration
From poisoning my body

- *drunk*

Can we pretend
just for one day
that you're alive
i never lost you
i never cried
i never let your body
turn into ashes

Can we act like
you're still here
you come home
you miss me
you hug me
you're mad
about something

i'm tired
so exhausted
petrified
of knowing
i had you
your love
and I lost it

- tired

I sit here
High on my pedestal
Watching people die die die

I'm up here
Living and breathing
Smiling and succeeding
And all they do is die die die

I'm waiting
For another
soul breaking view
But I'm safe
I'm lucky
I'm comfortable
While they won't stop
They just die die die

Mothers and fathers
Children and lovers
Good people with futures
That will never happen

I'm begging the word
To stop
To take a break
Let me breathe
In between all the death

But the world keeps going
Even when lives
Are falling apart

For society that doesn't talk
We surely quickly move on
From life shattering
Death

No matter if you smile or cry
They always die die die
And just like that
Life passed us by

                        - *happy Tuesday*

I used to fear of dying
But if you could do it
So can I

- let's be together again

I was always an artist
A performer, an actress
But only loving you
Made me a writer

Missing you moved my soul
Every struggle wrote a poem
My heart overwhelmed with love
On the worst days
your words kept me going

But not until your death
I got on the stage
And slammed my heart away

Your love made me a writer
Your death made me a poet
It is quite sad if you think about it
How much beauty
There is in a heartache

- your love made me a writer

Are you sure you're gone?
Because in my dreams you keep coming back
I just saw you last night
We picked a middle name for our future daughter
You seem so real every time
How can it be only in my mind?
If you're not planning on being alive
Please stop playing with my heart

- denial

People die every day.
Just like you every morning
When my dreams fade away.
If you can't choose to stay
I don't care about all the glory
I'm okay with ending my story.

- happy ending

I dare the world to kill me
the way it killed you.
But why would it start listening to me now?

- prayers

I couldn't believe how lucky I was.
And I wasn't.
You were given to me
Just to be taken away.
Being your wife is the best
And the cruelest thing that has ever happened to me.

- *that lucky*

When you look at me…
What do you see?
A cute girl, a redhead, big smile, nice body…
It's so easy to miss, all the trauma underneath.

Unfortunately, I belong to a secret club.
Not by choice, I was forced by the world.
The Dead Husband Club is a secret well-kept by our society.
You don't know of its existence until you have no choice but to
face the reality.

You know how it goes. You meet a guy. You fall in love. You
get married, maybe have kids. Then he dies before his time and
fuck… you didn't sign up for this.
No one ever told us husbands die in their twenties. No one said
"till death do us part" might happen before you even notice.
We all are way too fun, too young, and too hot to bury the ones
we loved.
We fell in love expecting forever and all we got are heartbreaking
memories.
We dressed for funerals before our wedding gowns got dusty.
Our wedding rings didn't even have a chance to get rusty.
We got married and said goodbye to dating. Just so we could get
back to where we started a few years earlier.
Only now we're slightly older and wiser.
With paralyzing trauma and dead husband nightmares.

People can't decide whether we are women or just widows.
Whether they should hit on us or deem us unfuckable.
We're hot, yet damaged. Young, but lived the lives of many.

We got our power from putting together broken pieces.
There will always be parts of our hearts missing.
We all are too hot to be young widows.
People mistake our loss for newly gained freedom.
But in this cruel world of grief
We found each other.
And every single day
We help yet another
Widow…
To breathe…

- too hot to be a widow

I don't think I even remember how it felt to be yours
It seems so distant that I'd believe if someone told me I never was
What do I owe you?
A lifetime of grieving?
Tears down my checks for eternity?
Living my best life and making you proud?
What do you want me to be?
Dead inside or happy to be alive?
I'm having trouble figuring this grief situation out.
I'm not sure what I'm feeling and how to let everyone know I'm
still your wife.
I'm frustrated and broken
But your death showed me life is too short
To leave things not lived through or unspoken.
I'm doing my best to share you with people
But you never even wanted to be that visible.
So how do I stay married to the love of my life
While you're not here and I'm just 27 - taking on the world?

- a bus ride to Masaya

I'm just waiting for another death.
Which one will come first?
Mine, or everyone else's?

- waiting

I was born to love you
I can feel it in my soul
it stings in my bones

But then life came into play
and I didn't get to learn
how to do it well

Not until you left
I learned how immense
our love became

Now it's too late
some might say
but I see it in a different way

I had you
then I lost you
and while it is a tragedy

I had you
and that's so much more
than many will ever have

I'm broken
but I'm grateful
beyond my understanding.

- beyond

your love
made me
your love
lifted me up
your love
drove me crazy
now your love
is breaking
me apart

we were
young
we were
different
we had
something
to prove
we failed
but it was
worth it

every second
every minute

- youth

10 year plan

When I tell people, very rarely do I tell this to anyone, I know they think that I'm crazy... I can see it though. I see it so clearly. One day, hopefully no later than in about 10-12 years, we will be back together again. I can see you standing at the gates of heaven waiting for me with a smile on your face. We are both dressed in white, you look as beautiful and young as the last time I saw you. Everything around us is bright. You are waiting for me… and as soon as I approach you, I'm back in your arms again. And that's where I stay. And nothing else matters. But maybe we get to live another life and I get to find you and fall in love with you all over again… I really hope that happens. That I get to live many lives of falling in love with you and each time is going to be just as breathtaking as this one was. That would be a true happy ending. Because our love is too immense to fit into a lifetime.

in between

One
She learned to walk
Two
She started to talk (a lot)
Three
Turned into a wild child
Four
Lied her dad was a stranger so she could keep playing with her
friends
Five
Started liking the boys
Six
Made out with a boy from kindergarten
Seven
Thought she was a grown up
Eight
Had her first summer fling
Nine
Fell in love with the freedom on a summer camp in Spain
Ten
Watched too many teenage shows
Eleven
Changed schools for really no reason
Twelve
Went to Turkey and saw mountains meeting the sea
Thirteen
Had her first beer
Fourteen
Had her first cigarette (and many more)

Fifteen
Blacked out and her brother dragged her home
Sixteen
Realized people are nicer to girls with eating disorders
Seventeen
Fell in love with her best friend (both of them)
Eighteen
They broke her heart and she got fat
Nineteen
She went to see the world
Twenty
She got her dream job
Twenty One
Learned you don't drink at office parties and hook up with
coworkers
Twenty two
Accidentally met her soulmate
Twenty Three
Got married to the above
Twenty Four
Young, married and poor
Twenty Five
Everything came together
Twenty Six
Bring it on!

- 26

I want to keep this poem
And hold it to my heart
As proof
Someone knows me

- Rupi Kaur knows me

Young
Married
Quarantined.
Away from family
Away from everything.
While inside the bubble
It all seems to be fine
But outside of the bubble...
Wait... is there outside?
My best friend
Across the ocean
My family
Even further.
It's been years
And I'm not any closer.
I chose love
I chose to stay
It was my choice
I can't complain.
But I miss them
I miss there.
I miss those places
That I used to call home
Back in a day.
I'm away.
What more can I say?
I'm home
But where is it?

She's busy...
She won't even visit.
She can't,
I know.
The borders are closed
And I'm here alone.
I'm away.
What more can I say?

- away

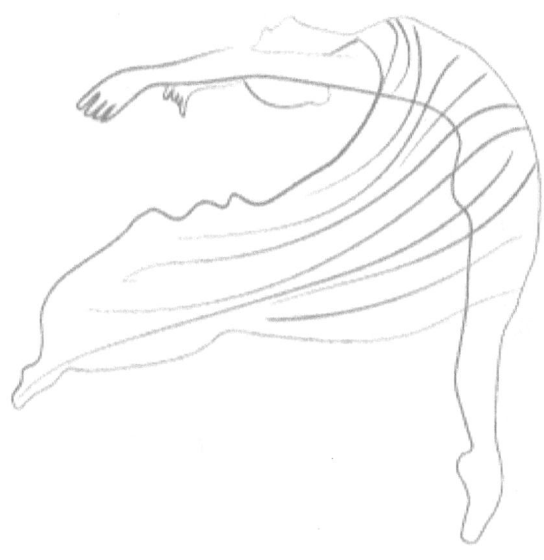

sitting in a bright room
lit up with artificial lights
ugly office chairs
boring artless art

creativity dying
minute by minute
my soul crying
begging for freedom

one day I'll be out
of this grey
corporate world
I'll put colors in my life
surround myself with
abundance of joy

until then I'll be here
writing poems
they'll never see
about what I hope
to make
my life be

- friday at the office

People say
You can't just pack and go.
People say
You can't drop everything
to follow your dreams.
But as soon as I dip my toe
I want all of this
I want a life that's so beautiful
it brings me to tears.
So why can't we?
What's holding us back?
Mortgage
Rent
Pets
Children
We make ourselves slaves
And suddenly there's no way out.
Beautiful things
Beautiful home
Beautiful children
Beautiful dogs
We all want that beautiful life
But where's the beauty to me?
Outside.
Stepping on the tight rope
Balancing
Tripping
Looking for a way out.
I want all of it.
How crazy am I?

I want the house
with a picket fence
I want a porch
filled with pumpkins
that turn into a snowman.
I want dogs
resting on my legs
I might even want a baby
to name after my old friend.
But then I want to live
to explore
to fly
to adventure
to be free
How difficult can it be?
They say
You can't just pack and go.
They say
You can't drop everything
to follow your dreams.
But I'm not ready
to close that door…
To give up on
Anything
To give up on
Me.

- the choice

One day
You'll remember
The girl
You used to know

She sat
In your chair
Like it was
Her own

She was bold
She was fire
Unstoppable
Desired

You wanted her
They wanted her
Her attention
Her words
Her gestures

But she wasn't yours
She wasn't theirs
She was no one's
She belonged to the city

And then
One day
She left
And the world was hers

It wasn't long
Before she was
Discovered

She was loved
She was desired
This time
She gave in
This time
She stayed.

She had people
To love her
To desire
To listen
To tame her fire

But today
She's back
And she belongs
To the city

She walks around
With her head high
She's in power

Just for a moment
She's back
She's on fire

Funny thing
Being loved?
Desired?
She's walking alone
And that's her power.

- london

Look me in the eyes
and tell me
You don't see
the sparks flying

That's okay
give me all the lies
I'll write poetry
about it

- I'll use you for my poetry

Unfortunately, we will always have a photo of the exact moment I started falling for you.

Unfortunately, there's no footage of me smashing glass bottles at the wall the very next morning.

- frustrated

Thank you for telling my friend how you feel about me.
Let me know if you'd like to hear my thoughts about it.

Just let me be furious with you
For saying all the right things
For being a good person
For respecting my boundaries

I wish you didn't make me feel
Like I'm too damaged for your taste
Like the only person who pulled us
Is now making you push away

If you're not interested
I get it, that's okay
But in that case
Let's stop this game

Because I feel like I'm your sin
Waiting to be committed
It's not fucking fair
So why won't we just quit it?

Because we can't?
Because we don't want to?
Tell me it's all in my head
So I stop questioning my sanity.
Is that what you do with all the other girls?
Or just the ones you can't have?

Everything was good
But last night something changed
Now I have all those feelings
I wish someone looked at me
And saw through all the heartache and pain
But hey… don't worry
I'm used to being people's mistake.

- fuck bro code

My friend
My beautiful soul
Why do you seem to forget?
You're so much more

You deserve a life
Filled with love
Passion
People who know
how to make you laugh

Please don't forget
Life's too short
To be misunderstood
But it's too long
To suffer through

My sister
You shine so bright
Your fire kept me warm
When mine went down

I hate to see
The way
your heart bleeds
Every time
They turn their words
Into daggers

I'm begging
Don't let them ever
Overshadow
Your light
You're so much more

You are my stars
my moon
and the sun

- to all women I love

She's filled with the darkness
That breaks apart
Into the moon
And the stars

She's dancing
Knowing there's
Darkness within her

She's reaching for the sun
Barely touching
But never close enough
To be filled with the light

She's dancing
Despite the
Darkness within her

Sun and moon
Day and night
The girl filled with the stars
Is long way gone

It's all just afterglow.
But she will keep on dancing…
Until she's back in his arms.

- dancing gypsy

Twenty Seven
Feels like pain in pleasure
Like everything I resist
The taste of your lips is almost gone
And I'm here alone
Embracing the world
With the silent scream in my head
Damn, only a year ago
So happy, so naive
Thought life was fair
That karma exists
That God is good and doesn't take hostages
So silly, really
People die right and left
Everyone simply forgets
They say love will never fade
But then no one ever chooses to stay
There's a reason the greatest stories are tragedies
Falling in love is not enough
To be an artist you must hurt
You bleed with stories
To the last drop
Until it's all there
You bled out
You no longer hurt
Now that's all you are
You became their art.

- 27

Too drunk for my own good
Too scared to make another step
I can't even look at you.
You kind of drive me insane.

They say you're no good
But I don't really care
I can't even look at you
I think I'm done with this game.

How did we even get here?
My feelings make no sense.
I'm perfectly fine on my own
This crush is not here to stay.

I can't even look at you.
Because I know exactly
What my eyes would say.

- crAsh

This shouldn't hurt
the way it does.
I don't know why
I can't stop crying.
I guess I didn't expect you
to be so reckless
with my heart.

I know all the reasons
I've got them engraved
in my mind.
I don't know what
I expected.
I guess I hoped a friend
wouldn't break me
just like that.

Believe me, I'll survive.
I'm used to a heartbreak.
But being around you
is too confusing.
I don't think you get
how bad it got.

So, I'm sorry...
I know I fucked up.
But now I've got to pick up
the pieces.
And I need to do it
on my own.

- how to ruin a friendship

She's an artist
She's emotional
Kind of delusional
She lets her feelings
Be in charge of her thoughts
Yesterday she almost forgot
That life is more than pain
But today
There's abundance of joy
The sun is shining
And she almost forgot
That she's suffering
That her artist soul
Is not going to leave this alone
And while yesterday is gone
And today she doesn't feel alone
There's always tomorrow
She's a griever
Sometimes it's impossible
To retrieve her
From the darkness
Of her fucking brain
That drives everyone insane
When she goes into yet another
Cycle of disdain
She's a woman
Conditioned to love
Everyone but herself

To praise the bodies
That are not hers
To be little
And unworthy
Because being big
And loud
Means being angry
And crazy
She doesn't even know
That she's fucking amazing
She's an artist
Pouring her soul
Onto paper
Fighting to make a living
With every compliment
They pay her
Forgetting
How every day
She sacrifices
Everything she has
Just so they could be
Entertained
She's a woman
She's a griever
She's a fighter
She will never
Be understood

Don't pretend like
You even know her
The artist soul
Is not meant to be known
Just stand back
Don't mind her
Look and admire
Her eternal fire
Because the truth is
She'll be here
Long after you're gone
Her art will carry on
Her soul will never leave
The world that
Refused to believe
In her worth
Little did they know
The real tragedy
Is not her life
It's the truth
She is art.

- she is art

Epilogue

I am lost. I have no idea where I'm going. My new life seems to be to overshadowing what we used to have. I don't know… You're still here. I still love you. At the same time being loved by you seems extremely lonely these days. I'm In Between. Between the dreams and the reality. Between love and lust. Between missing you and wanting someone to give me the love you can't give me anymore. The living and breathing love I'm longing for so badly. I crave somebody's touch I'm sorry but I do. Can you blame me? I'm fucking twenty seven. I'm alive. My body… is more than alive. Something shifted within me. And maybe it's because of him, maybe it's because of you or maybe it's just my body waiting for my mind to catch up. I don't know… For now I'm just In Between. And I'm desperately trying to believe… it's okay to be here.

Also by this author...

Green Card Marriage

or visit...

drewsbookstore.com